BEYOND "DEVELOPING"

Rethinking Economic Systems and the Future of Enterprise

Perumal Koshy

tdw

TDW Productions & Publishing

Title: Beyond Developing: Rethinking Economic Systems and the Future of Enterprise
Author: Dr. Perumal Koshy

ISBNs:
978-93-91828-75-2 (Paperback)
978-93-91828-83-7 (Hardback)
978-93-91828-53-0 (Digital Download and Online Edition)

First Published: 2026
Published by:
TDW Productions & Publishing

Publisher's Note:
The views and interpretations expressed in this book are those of the author and do not necessarily reflect those of the publisher. While every effort has been made to ensure the accuracy of the information contained in this publication, the publisher assumes no responsibility for errors or omissions, or for damages resulting from the use of the information contained herein.

TABLE OF CONTENTS

NOTE:

Several chapters in this volume draw upon articles originally published in Global SME News (www.globalsme-news.com) across various issues. These have been expanded and analytically integrated to present a cohesive and updated volume.

Introduction

Rethinking Development in a Changing World

For decades, the global economic vocabulary has been built around a simple classification: developed and developing. These categories have shaped policy frameworks, institutional priorities, and the aspirations of nations. Countries were expected to "graduate" from one category to another by following a presumed linear path—industrialization, financial deepening, and integration into global markets largely defined by Western systems.

But that framework no longer reflects reality.
The global economy today is not structured along the lines it was in the decades following the Second World War. The institutions that defined devel-

opment thinking—multilateral financial systems, trade regimes, and geopolitical alliances—were built in a specific historical context that has since shifted. Yet the language and assumptions of development have remained largely unchanged.
This book begins with a simple proposition: the term "developing nation" has outlived its analytical usefulness.

Across large parts of Asia, Eurasia, the Middle East, Africa, and Latin America, economies are no longer operating as peripheral participants in a Western-led system. They are shaping their own models of growth, governance, and technological adaptation. Countries once described as "developing" are now driving global demand, building digital infrastructure at scale, and designing policy frameworks that respond to their own structural realities rather than imported templates.

At the same time, several traditionally "developed" economies are facing structural constraints—aging populations, rising public debt, and stagnating productivity. These challenges do not diminish their importance, but they do complicate the assumption that development is a one-directional process with a fixed endpoint.

The shift underway is not simply about economic growth rates or GDP rankings. It is deeper. It concerns how economies organize themselves, how innovation is generated, and how societies respond to change.

This book brings together a set of essays—originally published in Global SME News—each examining a different dimension of this transition. While written at different points in time, the arguments converge around a common concern: the need to rethink development in light of present realities rather than inherited assumptions.

The chapters engage with three broad areas.
First, global economic shifts—particularly the emergence of a multipolar world where power and influence are no longer concentrated in a single region.

Second, technology and governance—how digital systems, automation, and new forms of regulation are reshaping economic coordination and reducing dependence on traditional bureaucratic structures.
Third, enterprise and ethics—the changing nature of organizational culture, with a renewed emphasis on trust, character, and the human foundations of economic activity.

A recurring theme across these chapters is the importance of state capacity and institutional adaptability. Development is not merely about income levels; it is about the ability of systems to deliver—whether in healthcare, education, or digital public goods. It is about how effectively economies can integrate technology and create sustainable opportunities for their populations.

The essays in this book do not attempt to present a single, unified theory. Instead, they offer observations and reflections drawn from different contexts—policy discussions, technological change, and shifting labour markets. Taken together, they point toward a broader conclusion: the world requires a new vocabulary of development—one that recognizes diversity in pathways and focuses on outcomes rather than labels.

Retiring the term "developing nation" is not about semantics. It is about moving away from a framework that no longer explains how economies function or how progress is achieved.

The question is no longer which countries are developed or developing.

The question is which systems are capable of delivering resilience and inclusion in a changing world.

Part One

Beyond "Developing": Rethinking Economic Systems

The End of the "Developing World" Narrative

The first four chapters of this book examine the changing contours of the global economic order, moving beyond the traditional "developed vs. developing" distinction toward a more multipolar and dynamic reality. Together, they explore how shifts in state capacity, technological advancement, and enterprise behaviour are reshaping both global leadership and economic outcomes.

Rethinking Development: Chapter 1 questions conventional definitions of "advanced" economies, highlighting how countries such as Brazil, Russia, India, China, and South Africa are demonstrating strengths in areas like human capital, education, and institutional resilience.

Shifting Economic Power: Chapter 2 focuses on the ongoing redistribution of global economic influence, tracing the relative decline of traditional

Western dominance and the emergence of alternative frameworks in trade, finance, and cooperation. Emerging Multipolarity: Chapter 3 looks ahead to a world where economic and political influence is more widely distributed, with new centres of activity and dialogue emerging across regions.

Enterprise and Values: Chapter 4 brings the discussion to the level of firms and entrepreneurs, emphasizing that long-term success depends not only on capital or scale, but on discipline, trust, and value-driven leadership.

Taken together, these chapters present a grounded view of a world in transition—where both systems and behaviours are evolving simultaneously.

1

Why BRICS Nations Are the Real Advanced Economies Today

Time to Retire Developing Nation

Innovation, State Capacity & Resilience: The New Pillars of Global Leadership.

For decades, global development discourse has relied on outdated binaries—"developed" and "developing"—shaped by the post-World War II institutional architecture and Cold War geopolitics. The transatlantic powers of North America and Western Europe have long assumed the role of global standard-bearers of development. However, a closer look at present-day realities reveals a different story. On key indicators of state capacity, human capital, technological innovation, public service delivery, and urban resilience, the BRICS nations—Brazil, Russia, India, China, South Africa—and their expanding circle of partners are increasingly setting the pace.

Human Capital and the STEM Dividend

In human capital and education, BRICS countries exhibit striking gains. Russia maintains a literacy rate above 99%, with universities producing world-class engineers and scientists. China now leads globally in the number of STEM graduates, having rapidly reshaped its education system to meet the needs of AI, robotics, quantum computing, and biotech sectors.

India presents an equally compelling case. With over two million engineering graduates annually and a vast reservoir of medical and scientific professionals, it is fast emerging as a global talent powerhouse. Institutions like the IITs and AIIMS symbolize meritocratic excellence, with increasing outreach across socio-economic divides.

In contrast, several Western education systems face headwinds. Student debt, stagnation in math and science performance, and shortages of critical skills have raised alarms. The United States, for example, has over 40 million adults with limited literacy, while Europe grapples with an ageing workforce and bureaucratic inertia in higher education.

Industrial Strength, Strategic Autonomy, and Innovation

Beyond talent, BRICS economies are leveraging this human capital to achieve strategic industrial autonomy. Russia's defense-industrial sector has demonstrated resilience despite sanctions, sustaining production efficiently. India's push for self-reliance through "Make in India" is bearing fruit, including breakthroughs in space technology and defense exports. China, meanwhile, has become a global leader in electric vehicles, semiconductors, renewable energy, and advanced manufacturing.

These nations are no longer passive adopters of Western innovations. Rather, they are incubating their own technology ecosystems. India's Unified Payments Interface (UPI), China's AI deployments in healthcare and transport, and Russia's homegrown software solutions highlight the emergence of innovation models that are adaptive, context-specific, and strategically autonomous.

Healthcare Delivery: An Indicator of State Capacity

Healthcare, a litmus test of effective governance, tells a similar story. Western systems—often lauded for their sophistication—are increasingly beset by rising costs, service delivery challenges, and declining accessibility. Millions in the United States remain uninsured or underinsured, while public systems like the UK's NHS are overburdened.

In comparison, BRICS countries have made notable strides. India's healthcare sector combines public-private partnerships to offer quality care at globally competitive costs. China's AI-driven diagnostics and community-level care delivery are improving access in rural provinces. Russia's universal healthcare legacy continues to guarantee basic services across vast geographies. These systems, often marginalized in Western assessments, demonstrate greater cost-efficiency and broader outreach.

Urban Housing, Inequality, and the New Metropolis

Urban housing and inequality are further areas where BRICS nations challenge prevailing narratives. While homelessness and housing crises are becoming endemic in Western cities, many BRICS urban centers—despite structural challenges—have retained more inclusive housing access.
For instance, Russia's state housing programs continue to serve millions. In India, informal settlements, while lacking in amenities, nonetheless offer social cohesion, shelter, and proximity to employment—unlike the stark urban exclusion visible in encampments across Western metropolises. China's large-scale housing initiatives have transformed peri-urban zones into integrated urban habitats.

Though urban inequality persists, the architecture of social protection and shelter security is arguably more inclusive and accessible in many BRICS cities than in their Western counterparts.

Entrepreneurial Dynamism and Innovation at the Periphery

One of the most under-appreciated transformations is in entrepreneurial energy. India's startup ecosystem—supported by Aadhaar, UPI, and the Open Network for Digital Commerce (ONDC)—is fostering an innovation culture with local relevance. China's tech hubs in Shenzhen and Hangzhou are shaping global digital trends. Even under sanctions, Russia is fostering dual-use technology ventures and indigenous digital platforms.

Entrepreneurship in BRICS nations isn't mimicking Silicon Valley—it is evolving through frugal innovation, agile experimentation, and contextual problem-solving. These economies are producing scalable, resilient business models tailored to domestic challenges, often with global implications.

Emerging Global Centres of Gravity

BRICS countries are also becoming epicenters of global discourse. Their cities host leading business forums, summits, expos, and cultural festivals. From AI summits in Shanghai to G20 leadership in Delhi, these nations are increasingly anchoring global conversations.

Today, cities like Dubai, Delhi, Cape Town, São Paulo, and Shanghai attract comparable—if not greater—business and event footfall than many long-established "global cities" in the West. The geography of influence is shifting.

Development Reimagined

The West's claim to developmental supremacy was historically built on financial dominance, colonial extraction, and global institutional control. Post-war prosperity in Europe and North America, often mistaken for intrinsic superiority, was enabled by systemic imbalances in labor, capital, and trade. That paradigm is now unraveling.

BRICS nations are not simply "catching up." They are restructuring the fundamentals of development. Their urban centers, institutional frameworks, and productive capacities increasingly reflect the defining traits of advanced economies—adaptability, innovation, inclusion, and strategic autonomy.

As the West confronts mounting internal challenges—from debt burdens and industrial decline to political polarization—the world must recalibrate its assumptions. The global South, led by BRICS+, is no longer on the margins of development. It is the new frontier of dynamism and leadership.

The first world is no longer a geographic construct rooted in the West. It is a function of energy, creativity, state capacity, and societal resilience. In these domains, BRICS nations are not just participating—they are leading.

2

The Biggest Global Economic Shift in a Century is Happening NOW!

The transatlantic alliance is no longer the pillar of global economic power. Once dominant, it now struggles with stagnation, while emerging economies reshape trade, finance, and diplomacy in a multipolar world.

For decades, the world was defined by the economic and geopolitical dominance of the United States and Western Europe. Today, that order is unraveling. Power is shifting—not just eastward, but southward, as BRICS nations emerge as the new centers of economic and political gravity.

The Decline of Western Economic Dominance

The numbers tell the story. Europe's share of global GDP has plummeted from 21% in 1980 to 14% in 2023. Germany, once the industrial engine of the EU, is battling recession risks and losing competitiveness to China. France faces economic stagnation and political volatility. The UK, post-Brexit, is struggling to find its footing. Meanwhile, Western economies grapple with an aging population, declining productivity, and stagnant growth.

In contrast, BRICS nations—Brazil, Russia, India, China, South Africa, and new entrants like Saudi Arabia and the UAE—are expanding. They represent nearly half the world's population and 35% of global GDP (PPP). While the West tightens its grip on outdated financial structures, BRICS is building alternatives. The New Development Bank (NDB) has approved $32 billion in loans, bypassing Western-led institutions like the IMF and World Bank. Trade within BRICS is flourishing, with India doubling its oil imports from Russia, shifting transactions away from the dollar.

The End of Eurocentric Diplomacy

Diplomatic power, too, is shifting. When the US and Russia held recent back-channel talks, they did not meet in Geneva or Vienna—but in Riyadh. The Middle East, Africa, and Asia are no longer passive players in global affairs; they are actively shaping diplomacy.

For decades, the US and Europe dictated global negotiations through NATO, the G7, and Bretton Woods institutions. Today, these structures increasingly look like relics of a bygone era. BRICS nations no longer seek validation from Washington or Brussels—they are building parallel frameworks for trade, finance, and security.

A Post-Western Economic Order

The idea that the US and Europe remain the center of global economic power is obsolete. The G7 is no longer the engine of growth—BRICS is.

- China's economy (PPP) is already 30% larger than the US.
- India is set to overtake Germany as the world's third-largest economy by 2027.
- Russia's resilience against Western sanctions proves BRICS nations can bypass Western financial controls.
- Brazil's trade with China reached $157.5 billion in 2022, reducing its reliance on the US.

The transatlantic alliance is no longer the foundation of the global economy—it is becoming a regional pact of stagnant economies.

What Should Washington Do?

The US still has leverage—but only if it adapts to new geopolitical realities rather than clinging to outdated Cold War alliances. Its traditional partners in Europe are no longer the drivers of global growth, and resisting structural shifts in finance and trade will only accelerate its marginalization.

A strategic recalibration is essential:

1. Engage BRICS Economies with Pragmatism, Not Confrontation – Viewing BRICS as a monolithic adversary is a mistake. These nations have diverse economic and strategic interests, and the US must find ways to engage them on common ground—whether through trade, investment, or technology partnerships. A rigid confrontational approach will only push them further toward alternative economic frameworks.

2. Adapt to De-Dollarization, Not Fight It – The shift away from dollar-based trade is irreversible. Countries are already settling oil, commodities, and bilateral trade in local currencies. Instead of futile resistance, the US should modernize financial diplomacy, ensuring that the dollar remains relevant in a multipolar financial system.

3. Pivot to Growth Markets, Not Stagnant Alliances – The economic epicenter has moved

to Asia, Africa, and Latin America. Clinging to Europe as the default strategic partner is a mistake—its influence is waning. The US must actively engage with emerging economies, recognizing that the real opportunities now lie within the same BRICS-aligned nations it has long sidelined.

Washington still has a window to act—but hesitation will cost it geopolitical relevance. The old order is fading. The G7 no longer dictates global economic policy. BRICS is redefining trade, finance, and diplomacy. The real question for Washington is not whether to engage with this new reality—but whether it will do so before it is too late.

3

BRICS Rising: The Multipolar World Order

What to Expect in the Decade Ahead

The emergence of a multipolar world order, amidst Russia-Ukraine conflict and BRICS group bloc is going to be reality. Increasing acceptance of BRICS and interests among many in the developing & emerging economies is significant for many reasons. What will be the shape of the things and how the world will look like by the end of this decade?

Many predicts that in the emerging global order, Russia, China, and India will play increasingly influential roles. As BRICS nations takes center stage, its implications for development and peace are significant. Already, we see Gulf nations forging closer ties with Russia. Within BRICS, China India are collaborating on matters of mutual interests, despite usual border disputes . The Russia-Ukraine conflict has accelerated the transition to this new world order. Saudi Arabia and Iran have initiated talks, and further collaboration is expected. The world will be different. The rules of the globalization can be different. International Trade, Economic Polies and Economic systems can be different for each region and need not aligned with the US or British or the West European style in the world order.

With Russia, China and India assuming a global leadership position and a weakened United States and Western Europe, the world may experience greater peace, reduced conflicts and increased prosperity. Following are some of the short term and medium term cosmetic changes that may witness in the new world order.

1. In the Middle East region, we can anticipate peace, stability, and enhanced social, cultural, and economic ties between nations. Trade between these nations will flourish, gradually dissipating mutual suspicion and war-like situations.
2. Likewise, the South Asian region has the potential to emerge as a bastion of peace. With stability achieved, governments can focus on de-

velopment, education, and sustainable practices, leveraging the resources available.

3. Russia, India, and China, drawing from their socialist pasts, possess expertise in planning and implementing successful methods such as public distribution systems. By applying artificial intelligence to public distribution and planning, these nations can collaboratively develop better resource allocation systems to address hunger and malnutrition.

4. As the global power dynamics shift, new cities in Asia, Africa, and Latin America will emerge as centers of discourse, replacing traditional hubs like Geneva, Paris, London, New York, and Bonn. New hubs will be Al-Matty, New Delhi, St. Petersburg, Beijing, Johannesburg, Rio de Janeiro, Dubai, Cairo …and such other cities in the emerging world. They will become gathering points for international discussions.

5. The landscape of global summits will get redefined: from the Davos Forum to the St. Petersburg Forum or Dubai Forum or Beijing Forum, or New Delhi Forum.

6. Peace and development summits will be hosted in Thimphu and Kathmandu or Muscat or Dubai.

7. Scholars and academia from China and India will convene more frequently at the emerging universities of Nalanda and Taxila.

8. Advanced and economically feasible technology transfers will facilitate development in Af-

ro-Asian countries.

9. Hunger, poverty and malnutrition may get quickly eradicated.
10. Racial discrimination prevalent in the labour market may get significantly reduced.
11. Higher and technological education can become more accessible and cost-effective.
12. Afro-Asian countries may witness increased educational collaboration with Russia, India, China, Brazil, South Africa and universities from Eastern Europe and Central Eurasia.
13. With advanced technology and expertise from Russia, China, and India, Gulf nations may get on the track of economic diversification that suits to their culture and other realities.
14. Global trade reforms get enhanced emphasis. World Trade Organization (WTO) and international trade rules may get rewritten to accommodate local and traditional industries, preserving local economies and ecosystems.
15. Significant reforms will also be implemented within the United Nations system, granting the BRICS nations a major role.
16. There could be an exodus of Asian tech professionals back to their home countries from the United States, European Union, and United Kingdom, contributing to the growth and development of their home countries.

In conclusion, the emergence of a multipolar world order, speeded up by the Russia-Ukraine conflict and the influence of the BRICS nations, is expected to reshape the global landscape by the end of this decade. This shift in power dynamics is predicted to result in a stronger role for Russia, China, and India on the international stage, while the influence of the United States and Western Europe may weaken. This new world order holds significant implications for development, peace, and cooperation. The potential changes in the emerging world order will result in peace in the Middle East and South Asia, resource allocation collaboration among Russia, India, and China, accessible education and technology transfers, reforms in global institutions, and the return of Asian tech professionals. This new world order has the potential to bring peace, prosperity, and inclusive global cooperation.

4

What Lies Between Success and Failure for Start-up Ventures?

The line between success and failure for entrepreneurs—particularly startup founders—is often blurred. It's not capital, visibility, or even a brilliant idea that determines longevity. It's character. Values. And the ability to remain grounded when success tempts ego and shortcuts.

Generational family-run businesses offer valuable lessons here. Many operate within a disciplined framework honed over decades—sometimes centuries—of experience. They've weathered cycles of boom and bust. They know not to overspend just because the balance sheet looks good. If a second car isn't essential, it's postponed. Decisions are measured, not reactionary.

More importantly, these businesses are built on trust and integrity. Financial prudence is only part of the equation. Success also means being a responsible human being. As Mahatma Gandhi said, business is an opportunity to serve—not just customers, but employees too. The most enduring enterprises treat their staff as partners, not overheads. Respect, belonging, and humility are embedded in their culture.

Contrast this with many modern startups, where even small wins are mistaken for world-conquering success. Ego inflates. Luxury purchases follow. Surveillance culture creeps in. Recently I came across a startup headquartered in the Gulf with offices in India. It began as a digital ad agency and saw quick success. The founder soon diversified into events, bought multiple luxury cars, and installed CCTV cameras across a small office. Employees leave within weeks. Micromanagement rules. Leadership is autocratic.

Compare that to a modest family-run firm, which again, operating in the same sector in the same city, run by South Asian entrepreneurs in the Gulf region. No CCTV. No spy software. No mass attrition. Just a culture of trust and shared goals. Employees stay because they're respected. They work as a team—and a family.

Some startup leaders believe success is built through relentless pressure. Recent comments by leading industry veterans advocating for 70- to 90-hour workweeks reflect this mindset. It's a flawed argument. Evidence shows that consistently working beyond 48 hours leads to serious health risks and burnout. Development doesn't come from exploitation—it comes from balance.

The startup world must rethink its culture. Surveillance, overwork, and fear-driven management don't scale. They burn out talent and corrode trust. High attrition isn't a sign of growth; it's a symptom of dysfunction.

Technology and capital cannot compensate for toxic leadership. Sustainable entrepreneurship is built on ethics, empathy, and emotional intelligence. You don't build enduring ventures by squeezing the last drop out of your team—you build them by inspiring trust and walking together.

The real differentiator between success and collapse is not the size of your funding round—but the size of your values.

Part Two

Technology & Governance

Part II examines how digital transformation is reshaping the relationship between the state, markets, and individuals. As economies become increasingly data-driven, questions of governance, regulation, and ethics move to the centre of development discourse.

This section brings together perspectives on how technology is not only improving efficiency, but also redefining power, control, and accountability within economic systems.

AI and Economic Systems: Chapter 5 explores the role of artificial intelligence in shaping market behaviour, assessing its potential to enhance efficiency and transparency while raising concerns around excessive control and loss of human agency.

Regulation and Efficiency: Chapter 6 focuses on the use of digital tools to reduce bureaucratic complexity, highlighting how technology-enabled governance can lower compliance burdens and support more dynamic business environments.

Inclusion in Global Markets: Chapter 7 addresses structural disparities in labour markets, emphasizing the need for trade and policy frameworks that ensure fair access, mobility, and equitable participation. Workplace Ethics and Culture:

The concluding chapters turn to enterprise practices, examining issues such as surveillance, overwork, and control, and advocating for more balanced, trust-based approaches to managing people and organizations.

Together, these chapters reflect a central concern: as technology reshapes economic systems, the challenge is not only to adopt it, but to govern it in ways that remain efficient, inclusive, and humane.

5

AI as the New Invisible Hand: Can Algorithms Create the Ultimate Free Market?

For centuries, economic systems have depended on human decision-making, regulatory institutions, and ideological frameworks to manage resource allocation, production, and distribution. Capitalism uses market forces, socialism depends on planning, and mixed economies attempt a balance. But a new paradigm is emerging—AI-driven economic governance—where supercomputers and real-time data analytics play a central role in optimizing efficiency, enforcing transparency, and reducing economic distortions.

Can AI become the 21st-century 'Invisible Hand'—a more advanced and precise version of Adam Smith's concept—ensuring a self-regulating, bias-free economy? Or does it risk creating a system that erodes human agency and stifles innovation?

Soviet Cybernetic Planning: A Lost Opportunity for AI-Driven Economy

The concept of an AI-driven economy has roots in past attempts to use computational models for centralized economic planning. One of the most ambitious projects was the General State Automated System (OGAS), proposed by Viktor Glushkov in the 1960s. OGAS aimed to create a nationwide computer network to dynamically update economic plans based on real-time data from enterprises and consumers.

However, despite its potential, OGAS largely remained a theoretical endeavor, facing resistance from the Soviet bureaucracy, which feared a loss of political control over economic planning. Additionally, technological constraints and inaccurate data reporting from enterprises made implementation impractical. The project was ultimately abandoned, reinforcing the limitations of central planning in an era when real-time data processing was not yet feasible.

AI as the Supercomputer-Regulated Market Force

Traditional markets suffer from inefficiencies, information asymmetry, and bureaucratic delays. AI can potentially eliminate these distortions by:

- Real-time monitoring to detect supply-demand imbalances and optimize resource allocation.
- Automated regulatory enforcement, ensuring businesses comply with taxation, trade laws, and corporate ethics.
- Bias-free decision-making, removing human favouritism in licenses, permits, and government contracts.
- Monitoring and strict enforcement of labor laws
- Ensuring that environmental standards, worker rights, and fair labor practices are upheld in real-time.
- Large-scale interconnected AI networks that continuously assess compliance across industries, preventing exploitation and reinforcing ethical business operations.

By continuously analyzing economic data, AI ensures that markets remain efficient, fair, and corruption-free. Unlike centralized planning failures of the past (e.g., the Soviet Union's OGAS system), AI offers decentralized, adaptive planning that evolves in real time.

Can AI Ensure Market Inclusion and Fairness?

One of the biggest challenges in global economies is market exclusion, where small businesses and marginalized communities struggle for fair access. AI can:

- Automate digital credit scoring, enabling financial inclusion for unbanked entrepreneurs.
- Eliminate hiring and lending biases, ensuring decisions are based on merit, not privilege.
- Predict and prevent economic crises, allowing governments to act before recessions deepen.

If implemented ethically, AI can create a market that is not only efficient but also equitable.

Ethical Risks: The AI Economy Needs Guardrails

- However, AI's dominance in economic decision-making raises a number of fundamental ethical concerns:
- Threat to Human Autonomy – Will AI limit innovation and entrepreneurship by automating too many economic functions?
- Corporate and Government Overreach – Can AI-driven economies be manipulated by tech monopolies or authoritarian governments?
- Algorithmic Bias – Even AI can reinforce inequalities if its training data carries historical biases.
- Lack of Accountability – Who governs AI? Governments must implement AI ethics boards and transparent regulations.

The Future: AI as an Enabler, Not a Controller

Rather than replacing human decision-making, AI

should serve as an economic enabler—enhancing transparency, eliminating corruption, and ensuring fairness. Policymakers must strike a balance: Use AI for market regulation, not market domination. And ensure human oversight in AI-driven economic policies. Further, its important to develop legal frameworks to prevent monopolization of AI-driven decision-making.

AI has the potential to revolutionize economies, but its success will depend on how we regulate, programme, and govern it. If designed for the collective good, AI could become the most powerful force for economic fairness the world has ever seen—but if left unchecked, it could lead to an era of algorithmic authoritarianism.

The question is no longer whether AI will shape the economy—it is who will shape the AI-driven economy.

6

Smarter Markets, Stronger Economies: AI-Driven Deregulation for the Digital Age

Breaking Bureaucracy: Technology-Driven Deregulation for the 21st Century

Deregulation, tax reforms, and pro-business policies continue to shape economic discourse worldwide. While governments across developed and emerging economies have undertaken significant regulatory reforms—ranging from the UK's post-Brexit adjustments to India's ongoing business compliance simplifications—the conversation around bureaucratic inefficiencies, compliance costs, and regulatory bottlenecks remains critical.

One of the most transformative levers of deregulation today is technology-driven governance. The integration of artificial intelligence (AI), digital governance, and automated compliance systems has the potential to streamline bureaucratic processes, reduce corruption, and enhance regulatory efficiency. Countries such as Estonia, Singapore, and the UAE have already implemented AI-driven tax administration, automated business registration, and digital licensing platforms, dramatically reducing compliance burdens for businesses and fostering a more competitive economic environment.

However, the debate is far from settled. While deregulation and technology-driven reforms have yielded positive economic outcomes in some regions, regulatory inefficiencies still stifle entrepreneurship, slow job creation, and restrict economic dynamism in many economies. The challenge now is to accelerate these reforms in a way that ensures tangible benefits for businesses and workers alike while balancing necessary regulatory safeguards.

As the U.S. moves toward another phase of economic policy shifts under Donald Trump, the ripple effects of its approach to deregulation, tax policies, and business incentives are likely to influence global regulatory frameworks. Will this drive a new wave of market-friendly reforms, leveraging AI and digital governance, or will it reignite concerns over corporate excesses and economic disparities? The coming years will be critical in shaping the future of global regulatory landscapes.

The Regulatory Burden: A Barrier to Entrepreneurship and Economic Expansion

Excessive regulation has long been a structural impediment to economic growth, particularly for small businesses and startups. Unlike large corporations that can absorb compliance costs, smaller enterprises often struggle under the weight of bureaucratic red tape. Complex licensing requirements, redundant compliance frameworks, and excessive labor laws create barriers that hinder market entry and innovation.

The impact is twofold: first, it discourages entrepreneurship by making business formation an arduous process; second, it diverts resources from productive activities, forcing firms to allocate capital toward compliance rather than expansion and innovation.

World Bank's Doing Business reports consistently highlight a direct correlation between regulatory efficiency and business competitiveness. Nations that streamline business regulations see higher levels of investment, greater entrepreneurial activity, and increased employment.

Deregulation as a Catalyst for Growth

From a macroeconomic perspective, deregulation aligns with supply-side economic principles advocated by Milton Friedman and Arthur Laffer. Supply-side economics posits that reducing regulatory burdens, lowering taxes, and minimizing government intervention can enhance economic efficiency, incentivize investment, and stimulate long-term growth. Friedman argued that excessive regulation distorts market mechanisms, leading to inefficiencies and slowing productivity. (Capitalism and freedom, 1962). The economic impact of tax cuts is generally positive, as they stimulate economic activity, drive job creation, and boost production by incentivizing investment and consumer spending. According to Arthur Laffer's analysis in The Laffer Curve: Past, Present, and Future (2004), lower tax rates can lead to increased taxable economic activity, ultimately offsetting revenue losses and fostering long-term growth.These principles have influenced pro-business policy frameworks worldwide, particularly in economies seeking to enhance competitiveness and attract investment.

Reducing regulatory barriers enhances productivity, increases labor mobility, and ensures efficient capital allocation. Countries that adopt deregulation-friendly policies attract higher levels of foreign direct investment (FDI) and witness an uptick in job creation and wage growth.

Studies by UNIDO and the International Labour Organization (ILO) suggest that an overly stringent regulatory environment, if not carefully designed, can lead to unintended consequences such as higher unemployment and increased informality. In contrast, economies that implement targeted deregulation—such as simplifying business licensing, streamlining tax compliance, and easing labor market rigidities—tend to foster more dynamic economic activity.

Lowering compliance costs incentivizes capital expenditures, while tax incentives encourage firms to reinvest in expansion and workforce development. Robert Mundell has long argued that strategic tax reductions lead to higher economic activity, ultimately broadening the tax base and mitigating revenue losses in the long term.

Conversely, economies burdened with excessive regulation tend to experience capital flight, weaker job creation, and an expansion of informal business activities. A well-calibrated approach—one that removes inefficient regulations without compromising consumer and environmental protections—remains key to sustaining economic resilience.

Pro-Business vs. Pro-Market: Striking the Right Balance

The debate over deregulation is often framed as a business-friendly initiative, but a crucial distinction must be made between pro-business and pro-market policies. While pro-business policies may favor large corporations by reducing tax burdens and easing compliance requirements, they do not necessarily foster competition. Instead, deregulation should be structured as a pro-market strategy—one that enhances competition, lowers entry barriers for small enterprises, and prevents monopolistic practices.

Pro-business deregulation that disproportionately benefits large firms risks creating an uneven playing field, where dominant players entrench their market position at the expense of smaller competitors. A well-designed regulatory rollback should, therefore, prioritize policies that enhance market accessibility for startups and SMEs while preserving a competitive landscape.

Technology-Driven Deregulation: The Role of AI and E-Governance

A key lever for deregulation in the 21st century is the adoption of artificial intelligence (AI) and digital governance tools. Governments worldwide are increasingly leveraging technology to streamline compliance and reduce bureaucratic inefficiencies.

AI-driven tax administration, automated business registration, and digital licensing platforms can significantly cut regulatory delays, reduce corruption, and lower operational costs for businesses.

For example, AI-powered tax systems can automate compliance procedures, enabling businesses to file returns with minimal paperwork. Predictive analytics can enhance fraud detection, eliminating the need for intrusive and time-consuming manual audits. Digital governance tools can also expedite business licensing, making it easier for entrepreneurs to navigate regulatory processes without the traditional hurdles associated with bureaucracy.

Toward a Balanced Approach to Deregulation

The key lies in a targeted, pro-market approach that eliminates inefficiencies while preserving essential protections. For global policymakers, the path forward should focus on:

1. Reducing barriers to entry for small enterprises and entrepreneurs who are starting up.
2. Leveraging technology to enhance regulatory efficiency and transparency.
3. Streamlining tax and compliance frameworks to promote investment.
4. Ensuring that deregulation does not translate into monopolistic advantages for large firms.

As governments navigate the complexities of economic policy, one pressing question remains: Will regulatory frameworks evolve to sustain competitive entrepreneurship, or will deregulation disproportionately favor corporate incumbents? The answer will shape the future of global business dynamics in the years to come.

7

Why Free Trade Agreements Should Address Labor Market Disparities

Free Trade Agreements (FTAs) fuel economic growth by cutting tariffs and opening markets, yet they miss a critical inefficiency: labor market disparities tied to racial or ethnic factors that sap productivity and growth. Trade isn't just goods—it's the workers powering innovation and supply chains. When hiring biases and wage gaps limit talent based on demographics, economies lose billions—up to 4% of GDP in advanced nations, per the IMF. FTAs, designed to maximize prosperity, can't ignore this drag. Adjusting them to address these gaps could unlock significant gains in efficiency and output.

The Cost of Labor Market Gaps

Evidence highlights inefficiencies tied to these disparities. The International Labour Organization (ILO) finds migrant workers—frequently from minority backgrounds—earn 13% less than nationals in high-income countries, a gap not fully explained by skills or qualifications. In the US, McKinsey's 2021 analysis notes Black professionals with comparable credentials face a 20-25% wage differential, with only 5% reaching senior roles despite representing 13% of the workforce. The UK's 2022 TUC survey reports a 12% median pay gap for Black and Minority Ethnic (BME) workers, alongside recruitment challenges. The EU's 2020 Eurobarometer data shows 33% of ethnic minorities perceive bias in job applications, while Australia's 2023 Diversity Council finds Asians and Africans with advanced degrees are 30% less likely to secure interviews, earning 15% less when hired.

High-skill sectors illustrate the issue starkly. Indian IT professionals, critical to tech economies, earn €15,000 annually in Germany versus €75,000 for locals (OECD 2022), and $80,000 in the US versus $150,000 for domestic peers (BLS 2023), despite equivalent expertise. This wage suppression limits the mobility of talent that modern trade systems depend on, creating inefficiencies rather than competitive advantages.

The Economic Opportunity

Addressing these gaps offers substantial gains. The IMF estimates that reducing labor market disparities could boost GDP by 2-4% in advanced economies—potentially $1 trillion annually for the US. The ILO's 2023 Global Wage Report suggests Germany loses €30 billion yearly in productivity as skilled migrants pursue better opportunities elsewhere. A 2020 World Economic Forum study ties diverse workforces to a 19% increase in innovation revenue, an edge diminished by exclusionary practices. In the UK, the 2021 Parker Review shows FTSE 100 firms with diverse boards outperform peers by 3.5% annually, though ethnic minorities hold just 13% of director roles. In the US, Black-owned firms added $183 billion to GDP in 2022 (McKinsey)—a figure that could grow with equitable access to trade resources.

Critics argue that markets naturally resolve wage differences through competition, attributing gaps to visa policies or negotiation leverage rather than bias. However, a 2023 Harvard Business Review study finds résumés with African or Asian names receive 50% fewer callbacks than identical ones with white-sounding names—a pattern consistent since 2004. This suggests structural barriers, not just market dynamics, are at play.

Corporate Insights

Surveys underscore these inefficiencies. In the UK, 60% of BME workers report promotion barriers (TUC 2022). The EU's 2021 FRA survey finds 45% of Sub-Saharan Africans encounter hiring obstacles, with a 20% wage gap in tech. In Australia, Asian PhD holders earn 18% less than white peers (ANU 2022), while in Germany, Indian IT workers cite a "foreigner penalty" in pay (IW 2023). In the US, 55% of Asian tech workers link earnings caps to demographic factors (Pew 2022). These patterns signal untapped potential that FTAs could help unlock.

Enhancing FTAs for Efficiency

Current FTAs, like the USMCA or EU-India negotiations, address labor standards broadly but lack specific mechanisms to tackle these disparities. The USMCA's labor provisions, for instance, don't enforce wage parity or hiring equity. By contrast, the EU's Racial Equality Directive (2000) reduced hiring bias by 15% in member states (EC 2023), showing policy can drive change. FTAs could adopt practical measures:

- Standardize Pay Norms: Include "equal pay for equal work" guidelines linked to ILO benchmarks, with optional audits to monitor compliance.

The ILO projects this could reduce wage gaps by 10% in five years, narrowing disparities like those faced by Indian IT workers.

- Streamline Talent Mobility: Expand GATS Mode 4 to standardize skill recognition and reduce visa-related wage penalties, ensuring talent flows efficiently across borders.
- Support Diverse Suppliers: Encourage—rather than mandate—a target like 5% of supply chain contracts for minority-owned firms, mirroring World Bank success in South Africa, where Black exporters grew 25% since 2015.

The Broader Impact

Unresolved labor gaps risk disrupting global cooperation. India, a major source of US H-1B visa holders, and countries like Nigeria and the Philippines, key suppliers of healthcare workers, may redirect talent if disparities persist. UNCTAD's 2023 report warns human capital mobility could decline 20% by 2030 without action, costing tech $5 trillion and healthcare $2 trillion. Investors managing $40 trillion in ESG assets (Bloomberg 2023) increasingly prioritize equitable systems, suggesting FTAs that address these issues could attract more capital. Implementing such measures might raise trade costs slightly—audits could add 1% to expenses—but the economic upside far outweighs this. A more efficient labor market fuels growth; persistent

inefficiencies hinder it. FTAs have the potential to enhance not just trade in goods, but the human capital that underpins it. Policymakers should consider these adjustments to ensure trade agreements deliver their full economic promise.

8

Your CV Is Not Their Commodity

Rethinking Digital Hiring Ethics

In today's digital hiring economy, we seldom pause before uploading our CVs—often packed with personal details—to job portals, freelance platforms, or recruitment databases. But this seemingly routine act has quietly become a high-risk move. What should merely showcase our capabilities ends up revealing far too much: full contact details, scanned documents, ID numbers, and even family information.

Once shared, that data rarely stays in one place. It may be stored indefinitely, used to train algorithms, monetised by third parties, or worse—leaked into networks that enable fraud and impersonation.

Oversharing Is Not a Competitive Advantage
Throughout the hiring process, candidates are pressured to disclose more than necessary. Many job seekers comply, assuming it enhances their prospects. But companies that hire based on excessive data rather than actual capabilities are not hiring you—they're profiling you.

The reality is, employers who genuinely value your contribution don't need your life story or personal documents upfront. They look for skills, insight, and alignment—not invasive data points.

From Job Seeker to Entrepreneurial Thinker

The employment landscape is undergoing a quiet but profound transformation. Traditional large-scale operations are giving way to more flexible, platform-driven, freelance, and service-oriented models. Increasingly, work is delivered through collaborative systems involving independent professionals, micro-entrepreneurs, and nano-enterprise networks.

This new reality demands a shift in mindset: from being hired to positioning your skills as value. Your CV should present you as an investment—not a resource to be extracted. You are not selling your identity, personality, or private life to a company; you are offering capabilities that solve problems. If a platform or employer asks for extensive personal data before even evaluating your merit, it's a warning sign: question the process—and the company.

Hiring Platforms: From Opportunity Engines to Data Funnels

Many digital job platforms today operate less like gateways to opportunity and more like data harvesting machines. Numerous listings—particularly unverified ones—exist primarily to gather information at scale. Consent clauses are buried in unreadable terms and conditions; data retention policies are vague, and user control is minimal.

The result? Job seekers report an immediate surge in phishing attempts, spam calls, and targeted marketing after uploading their profiles. This is no coincidence—it is a consequence of a system that treats your professional identity as a commercial asset.

Not All Companies Deserve You

Let's be honest. Some companies—and not just fringe players—operate with a control-based mindset. They demand documentation before interviews, initiate background checks without consent, and rely on opaque internal systems to monitor workers. These are not the future.

Increasingly, such exploitative models—marked by surveillance, secrecy, and burnout—are collapsing under their own weight. Ironically, many family-run enterprises and cooperatives offer more enduring, transparent, and trust-based environments.

What Needs to Change in Recruitment

If we are serious about building ethical hiring ecosystems, several fundamentals must shift:

- CVs must be lean. Do not include personal IDs, home addresses, or scanned documents unless explicitly requested at a later stage—and only with a guarantee of responsible use.
- Platforms must enable real consent. Users should be able to control who accesses their data, how long it stays online, and when it should be deleted.
- Data expiry should be standard. Inactive or outdated profiles should be auto-deleted unless users opt to retain them.
- Employers must be verified. Fake job listings thrive in environments where recruiters are not authenticated or vetted.
- Hiring must centre on dignity. Ethical hiring is not about box-ticking compliance—it is about respecting human potential.

ILO Principles: An Underused Global Resource
Protecting workers' privacy and autonomy is not merely a regulatory concern—it is a matter of dignity. Institutions like the International Labour

Organization (ILO) offer robust frameworks for worker protection. The ILO's 1997 Code of Practice on the Protection of Workers' Personal Data emphasizes consent, transparency, and data minimisation.

Its broader Decent Work Agenda and conventions on fair treatment, occupational safety, and working conditions provide both a moral and legal compass for the evolving digital workplace. Yet these tools remain grossly underutilised—especially in platform-driven employment.

Protecting Privacy Is Strategic Choice

In this new era, safeguarding your personal data is not a luxury—it is an act of self-respect. It's also a strategic choice. Talent today is mobile. You can build ventures, freelance globally, or contribute across sectors without surrendering your digital footprint.

Governments, development banks, and enterprise ecosystems are increasingly supporting fair, sustainable, and ethically governed businesses. The digital economy rewards imagination, agility, and value—not blind compliance.

If a recruiter cares more about your passport than your portfolio, walk away. If your workplace thrives on surveillance or disrespect, take your skills elsewhere. If you're judged by your identity instead of your contributions—challenge it.

You owe nothing to a system that doesn't see you as a person. In reclaiming control over our data, we are not just protecting CVs—we are redefining what it means to be employed. The future of work belongs to those who value both opportunity and integrity.

A Call for Policy Action

Governments must act decisively to protect worker data in the digital age. This means enacting dedicated labour data protection laws that go beyond general privacy frameworks. These laws must regulate how CVs, employment histories, and personal identifiers are collected, stored, shared, and deleted.

In platform-based and gig economies—where formal contracts are often absent—these safeguards are not optional; they are urgent. Without them, hiring risks becoming a system of profiling, exclusion, and exploitation.

A rights-based approach to digital employment must now be embedded in every nation's labour policy and data governance strategy.

Part Three

The New Workplace

Part Three shifts the focus from broader economic and technological frameworks to the human and institutional realities of the present moment. It examines how these larger transformations are reshaping workplaces—across offices, boardrooms, and evolving labour markets.

A central concern in this section is the gradual emergence of a psychology of control within organizations. Chapter 9 explores how intolerance toward dissent and rigid leadership cultures can stifle innovation and mirror exclusionary tendencies seen in political systems. In such environments, adaptability becomes difficult.

The section also revisits the question of work intensity. The growing normalization of long working hours is often framed as commitment, but evidence suggests the opposite. Sustained overwork weakens productivity, creativity, and long-term performance. In this context, work-life balance is not a luxury, but a strategic requirement. Experiences from countries such as the UAE, Iceland, and New Zealand illustrate this shift.

Another key theme is the changing nature of hiring. Chapters 8 and 10 examine how recruitment processes increasingly function as mechanisms for data extraction rather than genuine talent identification. This raises concerns around privacy, consent, and dignity. The argument here is for a shift in mindset—from being treated as a resource to positioning one's skills as value.

Underlying these discussions is the role of institutional choice. Everyday decisions within firms—whether in management practices or consumption patterns—shape broader economic systems. Even choices such as adopting locally produced materials like Khadi can support more sustainable and labour-intensive production structures.

Taken together, this section argues that the future of work will be shaped not only by technology, but by the ethical frameworks within which it operates. The challenge is to ensure that evolving workplaces remain grounded in dignity, trust, and human agency.

9

Why Businesses Must Guard Against the Psychology of Control

Authoritarianism Begins at Work

In times of crisis or transition, the temptation to cling to certainty becomes dangerously appealing. But when certainty turns into absolutism—the belief that "whatever I think, believe, or say is correct, and only my version is valid"—we cross into the realm of authoritarian psychology. This mindset, at its extreme, has historically laid the foundation for Fascism and Nazism. It dehumanizes others, rejects dialogue, and glorifies control.

What we often overlook is that this tendency doesn't begin in political parties or state structures. It begins with a psychological posture—a refusal to accept complexity, contradiction, or dissent. It begins when leaders or institutions refuse to be questioned, when systems are designed to punish disagreement, and when criticism is treated as betrayal. In the 1930s, this was the fertile ground that nurtured fascist ideologies. In our own times, it quietly creeps into corporate boardrooms, media narratives, social media algorithms, and enterprise culture.

Absolutism in Business Leadership

Enterprises today operate in dynamic, complex, and often uncertain environments. While decisiveness is a key entrepreneurial trait, it must not morph into ideological rigidity. Many small enterprises, family-owned businesses, and even startups suffer when founders or decision-makers adopt a belief in their infallibility—resisting input, shutting down team feedback, or refusing to adapt.

Authoritarian business environments often:

- Penalize independent thinking;
- Reward blind conformity;
- Mislabel questions as disloyalty;
- Foster burnout through micromanagement.

This mirrors, in form if not in scale, the same exclusionary logic that totalitarian ideologies imposed on society at large: there is only one right way, and it is mine.

The Economic Cost of Intolerance

Whether in politics or enterprise, absolutist thinking is not just ethically troubling—it is economically unsustainable. Diverse teams, inclusive leadership, and open systems of knowledge-sharing are now recognized as key drivers of innovation. In contrast, rigid hierarchies and top-down control systems limit adaptability and resilience.

The authoritarian mindset is not compatible with a 21st-century economy that depends on collaboration, networks, and co-creation. And yet, many sectors—especially where digital transitions, generational shifts, or political interference are at play—show signs of a growing intolerance toward difference, criticism, or alternative models.

Reclaiming Humility and Dialogue

Whether in a political party, a public institution, or a small enterprise, humility is the first line of defense against fascism. It is the recognition that no one has a monopoly on truth, that progress comes through dialogue, and that leadership includes the ability to listen—and to admit error.

In the business world, this humility shows up in:

- Participatory management approaches;
- Learning organizations that embrace feedback;
- Policies that center inclusion over uniformity.

A pluralistic enterprise culture is not only morally necessary—it is vital for long-term survival.

Fascism begins in the mind long before it shows up in public life. When we declare others wrong by default, dismiss opposing views as threats, or shut down spaces of dialogue, we begin to mirror the same absolutist tendencies that fueled the worst ideologies of the 20th century.

Today, as we navigate volatility across economies, societies, and belief systems, we must ask: Are we building cultures of fear and conformity—or ecosystems of trust, dialogue, and shared futures?

The choice is not merely political. It is deeply personal, professional, and moral.

10

Why the Old HR Model No Longer Works

In today's rapidly evolving workplace, one fundamental question is rarely asked aloud but deeply felt across boardrooms and break rooms alike:
Is Human Resources as we know it dying?
The short answer is: yes—and it should be.

Traditional HR, with its roots in industrial-era management, is increasingly out of place in modern organizations. Once the gatekeepers of hiring, compliance, and control, HR departments are finding many of their core tasks—payroll, recruitment screening, onboarding—outsourced or automated. The "clipboard HR" of the past, obsessed with tracking time and surveilling workers, no longer fits the moment. If anything, clinging to that model risks organizational collapse.

Yet, while the old HR may be fading, a new HR is not only possible—it's essential.

The Wrong HR for the Right Age

In a world where companies are smaller, flatter, and more digital, the industrial-style HR model is showing its cracks. Surprisingly, some entrepreneurs launching startups today still bring in the old command-and-control mindset. They try to manage highly creative, knowledge-based teams the way one might run a factory floor.

This fails for a simple reason: people today don't want to be controlled—they want to be trusted.
We are entering an era where the term "employee" is giving way to "partner" or "associate." It's not just a linguistic shift—it reflects a deeper change in how work is done, and how people want to be treated. The newer generations—Millennials, Gen Z, and the emerging Gen Alpha—crave autonomy, psychological safety, and purpose. Surveillance tools masquerading as productivity apps, or micromanagement masked as "support," only erode trust and creativity.

The New Mandate: HR as Culture Builder
So what should HR do instead?

It must transform from monitor to enabler, from compliance officer to culture shaper. Technology can handle transactions, but it cannot manage relationships, empathy, or moral judgment. HR's future lies in designing frameworks where people feel seen, valued, and empowered.

Today's HR must:

- Build flexible, inclusive, human-centered work cultures
- Embed well-being and work-life balance into core values
- Mediate conflicts with emotional intelligence, not authority
- Prepare teams for AI-integrated futures through upskilling
- Guard against toxic surveillance disguised as accountability

This is not just an operational shift—it's a philosophical one. It means viewing people not as resources to be optimized, but as partners to be supported. It means recognizing that in the knowledge economy, how work is done matters as much as what is done.

From Function to Conscience

In many small or emerging companies, HR may not even exist as a standalone department. But the ethos of HR—the role of stewarding trust, fairness, and values—must still be present. Whether embedded in the founder's mindset or delegated to a people operations lead, this role is indispensable. In this new landscape, HR professionals—or their equivalents—must step up as custodians of ethics, dignity, and cultural integrity. They must help organizations scale values, not just rules.

A Necessary Death

So yes, HR is dying.

But what's dying is the outdated, hierarchical, transactional version of HR.

What's being born is something lighter, smarter, more relational—and far more human.

It's not the end of HR. It's the beginning of its real purpose.

11

Rethinking Work Hours

The Case for Balance in SME Growth Strategies?

Overwork is more than a health risk—it's a threat to productivity and sustainability, especially for SMEs. Studies by the WHO and ILO reveal that working 55+ hours weekly significantly raises the risk of stroke and heart disease, with 745,000 deaths linked to prolonged hours in 2016 alone. For SMEs, whose success hinges on human capital, chronic overwork leads to cognitive decline, impaired creativity, and absenteeism. The productivity paradox is clear: longer hours diminish critical thinking and problem-solving, undermining the very qualities that drive innovation and growth.

In the technology and knowledge-driven industries, the 70-hour workweek is often viewed as a badge of commitment and ambition. For small and medium-sized enterprises (SMEs) and their knowledge workers, the pressure to adopt such work patterns can be overwhelming. Tight deadlines, limited resources, and the drive to innovate often lead to extended hours. However, this relentless pursuit of excellence raises a critical question: Does the 70-hour workweek foster exceptional outcomes, or does it undermine the very foundations of growth, sustainability, and innovation for SMEs?

The Hidden Costs of Overwork

For SMEs, where resources are limited and every individual's contribution is vital, the costs of overwork are particularly severe. Prolonged working hours may initially seem necessary to achieve key milestones or scale operations. However, when entrenched as a norm, this approach exacts a heavy toll on employees' physical health, mental well-being, and productivity—qualities indispensable to knowledge-driven enterprises.

Medical research has consistently shown the dangers of overwork. A joint study by the World Health Organization (WHO) and International Labour Organization (ILO) (2021) revealed that working 55 hours or more per week increases the risk of stroke by 35% and ischemic heart disease by 17%. In 2016 alone, prolonged working hours were linked to 745,000 deaths from these diseases—a 29% rise since 2000.

These health risks translate into tangible costs for SMEs. Chronic overwork leads to diminished cognitive performance, impaired creativity, and higher absenteeism. Research published in the American Journal of Epidemiology and Current Cardiology Reports highlights that long hours exacerbate hypertension, cardiovascular issues, and cognitive decline. For SMEs, where human capital is the most critical resource, such outcomes are not just unsustainable—they are existential threats.

The Productivity Paradox

Contrary to the belief that "more hours equal more output," numerous studies reveal that productivity declines sharply beyond a certain threshold of work hours. Fatigue erodes critical thinking, decision-making, and problem-solving abilities, which are the cornerstones of success in IT and knowledge-based SMEs.

For SMEs, the stakes are higher than for larger organizations. Innovation in these firms often emerges from lean, focused teams, where every individual plays a critical role. Overwork risks burning out key contributors, leading to high attrition rates and stalling critical projects. SMEs cannot afford this loss of talent or momentum.

Balancing Work and Growth

In today's global economy, work-life balance is not a luxury—it is a strategic imperative. SMEs that prioritize employee well-being benefit from higher retention rates, improved morale, and enhanced creativity. For knowledge workers, in particular, balanced work environments foster the conditions needed for innovative thinking and sustainable productivity.

Governments and organizations worldwide are recognizing this shift. The UAE, for instance, has adopted a 4.5-day workweek for the public sector, encouraging private enterprises to follow suit. Countries like Iceland and New Zealand have also experimented with shorter workweeks, reporting improved productivity and job satisfaction. For SMEs in IT and knowledge-driven industries, these examples highlight a new pathway to achieving growth without overburdening employees.

Key Strategies for SMEs

To avoid falling into the 70-hour workweek trap, SMEs can adopt several strategies to balance work demands and employee well-being:

1. Flexible Work Arrangements: Offering remote or hybrid work options empowers employees

to manage their time effectively, reducing stress while enhancing productivity.

2. Outcome-Oriented Metrics: Shift the focus from hours worked to deliverables achieved. This approach encourages efficiency and innovation.

3. Wellness Programs: Provide access to mental health resources, ergonomic setups, and fitness opportunities to nurture resilience and reduce burnout risks.

4. Leadership by Example: Leaders should model balanced work practices, sending a clear message about the organization's commitment to employee well-being.

5. Automation and Technology: Invest in automation for routine tasks to free employees for higher-value, creative work.

A Call for Cultural Change

For SMEs, success in the knowledge economy depends on collaboration, creativity, and adaptability. Chronic overwork stifles these qualities, hindering innovation and long-term growth. The 70-hour workweek reflects an outdated paradigm that values effort over outcomes. For SMEs, the future lies in creating environments where well-being and innovation coexist.

By redefining success metrics, embracing flexible work models, and prioritizing sustainable growth practices, SMEs can position themselves as leaders in fostering innovation while retaining top talent. In an industry where human capital is the greatest asset, a thoughtful balance between productivity and well-being is not just an ethical choice—it is a strategic advantage.

The knowledge-driven economy demands a shift in mindset. SMEs that rise to this challenge will not only survive but thrive, achieving excellence without compromising the humanity of their workforce. Sustainable success lies in nurturing the best in both individuals and organizations.

12

Beware of Ghost Jobs

Why Fake Job Postings Are an Ethical Crisis

Are You Applying to a Real Job? Fake job ads—or "ghost job listings"—are on the rise, misleading thousands of job seekers every day. These deceptive vacancies waste time, harvest personal data, and erode trust in the hiring process

Sensitive data from CVs—combined with social media profiles—can enable phishing, fraud, identity theft, or even professional blackmail.
It begins with hope.

You find a job listing that feels perfect. The title fits,

the role sounds exciting, and the company is one you've long admired. You polish your CV, write a tailored cover letter, maybe even rehearse answers in your head. You hit "apply"—and then… nothing.
No reply. No update. After few days a system generated rejection letter. Sometimes, not even a rejection or response…

Weeks pass. The same job remains posted. Then you hear from someone inside the company: "Oh, that position? It was filled months ago." Or it could be some other answers..

There is a world of such fake job ads, world of ghost jobs—those enticing but empty listings that clutter our feeds and waste our time.

These aren't just harmless glitches in the hiring system. They're deliberate. And they're becoming alarmingly common.

Some companies claim they're "keeping their pipeline warm." Others say it's part of "future planning." But behind these vague excuses lies something far more cynical.

What's Really Going On?

1. Mining Data, Not Talent

Every job application is a goldmine of personal data—phone numbers, work history, even ID proofs. Some companies collect this not to hire, but to build databases. Marketing teams love it. So do third-party data brokers. And in shady corners of the internet, it's not hard to imagine where some of that information might end up.

2. Creating the Illusion of Growth

A company that appears to be hiring looks like it's thriving. A long list of openings signals success to investors, media, and competitors. But it's all theatre—recruitment as PR. The roles? Often imaginary.

3. Treating Applicants Like Research Subjects

Some job ads are nothing more than quiet market studies. What are people expecting in terms of salary? How rare is a certain skill? Instead of hiring experts, companies post a fake job and wait for the insights to roll in—for free.

4. Following the Rules (But Only on Paper)

There are also the jobs that were never open to the public to begin with. The internal candidate was already chosen, but HR posts it anyway—to tick compliance boxes or appear fair. The rest of the applicants? Ghosted.

What Job Seekers Lose

It's not just time. It's trust.

People spend hours preparing CVs, answering detailed questionnaires, sometimes even completing unpaid assignments—chasing roles that were never real to begin with.

For young professionals, especially in emerging markets, this cycle of silent rejection feeds burnout and self-doubt. You begin to question your worth. You wonder if you're doing something wrong.
But it's not you. It's the system that's broken.

Why This Has to Stop

Fake job ads aren't a clever strategy. They're a betrayal of people's time, energy, and dignity.

In an age where more people are freelancing, shifting careers, or trying to rebuild after layoffs, the idea of stockpiling CVs "just in case" is not just outdated. It's unethical.

Hiring should be honest. Grounded in real need. Driven by respect, not vanity metrics or shady surveillance.

Until that becomes the norm, job seekers must stay

sharp. Question early. Notice patterns. And trust your gut when something feels off.

Because a job post isn't just a form. It's a promise. And it's time employers took that promise seriously.

Part Four

Resilience and Regional Growth

Part Four shifts the focus to the practical engines of the emerging economy, examining how India is moving beyond a centralized, urban-centric model toward more balanced and regionally distributed growth.

At the centre of this transition is the rapid expansion of Micro, Small, and Medium Enterprises (MSMEs). Their exports have grown sharply—from about $47.4 billion to over $148 billion in a few years—while also strengthening regional economies and supporting higher-value production.

This shift is reinforced by targeted policy interventions such as the Pradhan Mantri MUDRA Yojana, which has expanded access to finance for micro-enterprises and enabled wider participation in economic activity. At the same time, structural constraints—particularly in state-supported systems—continue to slow reform and require careful attention.

The section also looks at the broader ecosystem needed for sustained growth, including support for labour-intensive sectors like Khadi and the potential of public institutions, such as libraries, to function as decentralized knowledge and enterprise hubs.

Taken together, this section argues that resilience in the modern economy will come not from concentration, but from distributed systems built on strong local enterprises and institutions.

MSMEs transforming India's Economic Landscape

India's Micro, Small, and Medium Enterprises (MSMEs) have emerged as a transformative force in shaping the country's economic future. Beyond their role in exports and GDP contribution, MSMEs have become a dynamic platform for fostering innovation, inclusivity, and regional economic integration.

Growth and Export Performance

Over the past few years, India's MSME sector has witnessed exponential growth. Exports from MSMEs surged from approximately $47.4 billion in 2020-21 to an impressive $148.7 billion in 2024-

25. This remarkable growth reflects an almost threefold increase in export value, highlighting the sector's expanding influence on international trade. Accompanying this growth, the number of exporting enterprises rose from 52,849 in 2020-21 to 1,73,350 in 2024-25, showcasing a significant enhancement in market participation. These achievements underscore the sector's critical role in strengthening India's trade competitiveness and integrating effectively with global value chains.

A closer examination of the sectoral composition reveals significant contributions across various industries. For instance:

- Textiles and Apparel: As one of the largest contributors, the textiles and apparel segment accounts for nearly 30% of total MSME exports. Products such as cotton fabrics, readymade garments, and handlooms are highly sought after in international markets, particularly in Europe and the US.
- Engineering Goods: This sector has seen rapid growth, contributing approximately 25% to MSME exports. Precision engineering products, including automotive components, industrial machinery, and electrical equipment, are key drivers.
- Pharmaceuticals and Chemicals: MSMEs in this segment are integral to India's global reputation as a major supplier of generic drugs and active pharmaceutical ingredients (APIs). The sector

contributes around 10% of total MSME exports.

- Handicrafts and Artisanal Products: Traditional crafts, including pottery, wooden artifacts, and jewelry, contribute about 5% to MSME exports, promoting India's cultural heritage on a global scale.
- IT and Digital Services: With the digital revolution, MSMEs have increasingly ventured into technology-driven exports, including software development, IT services, and e-commerce solutions. This sector, though relatively nascent, is experiencing exponential growth.

While these achievements reflect quantitative success, the qualitative aspect—such as fostering innovation, adopting digital technologies, and expanding market linkages—has been equally pivotal. Indian MSMEs have increasingly diversified into technology-driven exports, including IT services, precision engineering, and renewable energy products, enhancing their global appeal.

Resilience and Economic Stability

The MSME sector's contribution to India's GDP, rising from 29.7% in 2017-18 to 30.1% in 2022-23, highlights its integral role in economic stability. Even during the COVID-19 pandemic, the sector's gross value addition remained robust at 27.3% in 2020-21, rebounding to 29.6% in 2021-22. This resilience underscores the sector's adaptability in overcoming systemic shocks.

Key factors driving this stability include:

- Localized Production: MSMEs' proximity to domestic markets ensured the continuity of essential goods and services during crises.
- Digital Adoption: A surge in digital payments and e-commerce adoption enabled businesses to sustain operations despite physical restrictions.
- Policy Support: Timely interventions such as the Emergency Credit Line Guarantee Scheme (ECLGS) provided much-needed liquidity during the pandemic.

Driving India's Economic Transformation: The Role of MSMEs

As economies develop, there is a noticeable shift in resource allocation from agriculture to industry and services. This structural transformation reflects the changing dynamics of economic activities and productivity enhancement. Indian MSMEs exemplify this transition, with a growing emphasis on high-value manufacturing and service sectors. These enterprises not only adapt to evolving market demands but also serve as a bridge between traditional and modern industries, fostering innovation and competitiveness.

Through innovation and human capital development, MSMEs contribute significantly to long-term economic growth by promoting knowledge spillovers and nurturing entrepreneurial ecosystems. Their role in creating value chains, enhancing productivity, and generating employment is vital for sustainable development. Comparatively, economies in Southeast Asia and sub-Saharan Africa can draw critical lessons from India's MSME success story. By adopting sector-specific strategies that cater to local resources and market conditions, these regions can replicate India's achievements and accelerate their own structural transformation. This transition highlights the importance of targeted policy frameworks, access to finance, skill development, and infrastructure support to enable MSMEs to thrive in emerging economies.

Strengthening India's MSME Ecosystem: Policy Framework and Institutional Support

The growth of India's MSME sector is a testament to the country's robust policy framework and institutional support designed to empower small businesses. Recognizing the sector's potential as a cornerstone of economic development, the government has introduced a series of innovative policies and programs to address the unique challenges faced by micro, small, and medium enterprises. These initiatives focus on financing, skill development, infrastructure, and capacity building, creating an enabling environment for MSMEs to thrive and contribute significantly to India's GDP, exports, and employment.

Key Policy Initiatives Driving MSME Growth
1. Pradhan Mantri MUDRA Yojana (PMMY): A Game-Changer for MSEs

Launched in 2015, the Pradhan Mantri MUDRA Yojana (PMMY) has been instrumental in addressing the financing needs of non-corporate and non-farm micro and small enterprises (MSEs). By providing loans of up to INR 10 lakh, the scheme bridges critical funding gaps that often hinder the growth of small businesses.

- Shishu: Loans up to INR 50,000 for budding entrepreneurs to kickstart their ventures.
- Kishore: Loans ranging from INR 50,001 to INR 5 lakh for enterprises in the growth phase.
- Tarun: Loans between INR 5 lakh and INR 10 lakh for businesses seeking to scale operations.

This initiative has empowered millions of entrepreneurs, fostering economic inclusion and driving entrepreneurship across the country.
2. Revised Classification of MSMEs (2020): Incentivizing Growth

In a landmark move, the government revised the MSME classification in 2020, basing it on investment and turnover thresholds. This redefinition ensures that enterprises scaling their operations do not lose access to benefits and incentives, encouraging growth without penalties.

3. Skill Development: Preparing MSMEs for the Future

Programs like the Entrepreneurship and Skill Development Programme (ESDP) have been pivotal in equipping MSMEs with future-ready skills. These initiatives focus on areas such as digital marketing, automation, financial management, and product innovation, enabling small businesses to remain competitive in an evolving global economy.

4. Cluster-Based Development: Enhancing Competitiveness

The adoption of a cluster-based approach has proven highly effective for MSME growth. By fostering industrial clusters, enterprises benefit from shared resources, knowledge sharing, reduced production costs, and improved product quality. This collaborative model creates a competitive edge, particularly in sectors like textiles, handicrafts, and technology-driven manufacturing.

5. Financial Innovation: Expanding Credit Access

Access to credit remains a critical challenge for MSMEs, particularly for micro and informal enterprises. Innovations in financial support, such as collateral-free loans under the Credit Guarantee Fund Trust for Micro and Small Enterprises (CGTMSE), have significantly eased this constraint. Additionally, alternative financing models like crowdfunding and peer-to-peer lending platforms have emerged, offering underserved enterprises greater flexibility and accessibility to funds.

Building a Resilient Future for Indian MSMEs

India's policy initiatives demonstrate a comprehensive approach to addressing the multifaceted needs of the MSME sector. By focusing on financial inclusion, skill development, and fostering collaboration through clusters, these measures not only enhance the competitiveness of MSMEs but also position them as drivers of economic transformation. Moving forward, consistent policy innovation and institutional support will be key to ensuring that India's MSMEs continue to thrive in an increasingly complex and interconnected global economy.

Lessons for Developing Economies

India's MSME model offers several lessons for developing Afro-Asian economies:

1. Customized Policy Interventions: Policies tailored to local economic structures, as seen in India's sector-specific support, ensure inclusivity and scalability.
2. Technology Integration: Encouraging digital literacy and infrastructure development enables MSMEs to overcome geographical and logistical

barriers.

3. Public-Private Synergy: Partnerships with private players and international organizations can expand MSMEs' access to technology, markets, and capital.

4. Focus on Sustainability: MSMEs can lead the shift towards greener practices, positioning themselves as key players in the global sustainability agenda.

Challenges and Opportunities Ahead

While the Indian MSME sector has achieved significant milestones, challenges persist. Limited access to affordable credit, inadequate infrastructure, and market volatility remain pressing issues. However, these challenges also present opportunities for reform and innovation:

- Infrastructure Development: Investing in logistics hubs and industrial parks can reduce operational costs.
- Green Transition: Promoting renewable energy adoption among MSMEs can enhance energy efficiency and align with global sustainability goals.
- Global Collaboration: Participating in international trade agreements and global value chains can further enhance MSMEs' competitiveness.

India's MSME sector is not just a growth engine for the domestic economy but a blueprint for inclusive and sustainable development in the global south. By leveraging innovation, resilience, and policy support, MSMEs can address socio-economic disparities and drive regional integration. As developing economies seek to emulate India's success, adopting localized strategies and fostering cross-border collaboration will be critical to unlocking their economic potential.

14

Transforming Public Libraries into Creative-Knowledge Enterprise Hubs

Public libraries, vital in today's digital era, evolve beyond traditional roles into dynamic hubs for collaboration and innovation. They foster lifelong learning and cultural exchange. They have to evolve as shared workspaces for creators and entrepreneurs, leveraging existing infrastructure to boost economic growth. With India's extensive network of over 54,000 public libraries, converting them into coworking spaces addresses the challenges of workspace and technology access. By strategically allocating resources and establishing membership models for "shared workspace users", libraries become catalysts for knowledge-driven entrepreneurship. This transformation empowers enterprising youth and fosters economic prosperity, aligning with global trends in the knowledge and creative economy.

In the dynamic landscape of today's digitally driven knowledge and creative economy, public libraries can play a significant role. However, as knowledge resources such as books and journals become increasingly digitized, traditional public library visits are on the decline. Yet, these institutions retain their relevance as repositories of rare print materials and as public spaces for research and study. Recognizing their pivotal role, the UNESCO Library Manifesto of 2022 underscores the significance of public libraries in fostering lifelong learning, independent thinking, and cultural exchange.

Nevertheless, the potential of public libraries need not be confined to their traditional roles as quiet reading spaces. They have the opportunity to evolve into vibrant centers of collaboration, innovation, and knowledge-based entrepreneurship. Public libraries can emerge as shared working spaces for creators, gig workers, freelancers, and startup entrepreneurs, providing a launchpad for ventures even on a limited budget.

This transformation unlocks a plethora of opportunities for economic growth and job creation. In today's digital age, where information is readily accessible online, maximizing the utilization of public library spaces is imperative. By leveraging existing infrastructure and fostering collaboration, innovation, and entrepreneurship, local governments can cultivate a fertile ground for economic advancement, particularly in rural areas.

With the proliferation of high-speed WIFI and access to subscription-based scientific databases, public libraries can meet the diverse needs of the knowledge-driven economy. Strategic allocation of resources to enhance public library services can amplify their impact, enriching the lives of individuals and communities alike. Here repurposing community libraries into coworking hubs addresses the challenges of limited workspace and technology access, benefiting a large number of youth/gig workers/freelancers and creative-knowledge economy entrepreneurs aspiring to start knowledge-based and creative ventures.

However, to realize this vision, additional investment and space creation are needed. A working model and terms of reference for enterprise members should be established, with charges levied for facility usage. Unused library space can be converted with the necessary infrastructure, ensuring maximum utilization and revenue generation. Though charges for entrepreneur members may be lower than commercial rents, this model is mutually beneficial for the library movement and aspiring entrepreneurs alike.

India has an extensive network of over 54,000 public libraries. Out of this 54000, 12% or around 6400, are equipped with computers, while 8%, 4300, have access to the internet (Ministry of Culture, Govt.of India and UNESCO Institute of Statistic Report 2018).

Knowledge enterprises, driven by intellectual assets and innovation, are key drivers of economic progress and societal development. Collaborative efforts among policymakers, educators, and industry stakeholders are essential to create an enabling environment for innovation and creativity. Entrepreneurial ecosystem development, streamlined access to finance and funding, and supportive policies are crucial pillars for promoting knowledge economy entrepreneurship.

Transforming community libraries into coworking spaces serves as a catalyst for economic growth and empowerment. By bridging the digital divide, nurturing entrepreneurship, and enhancing local talent development, these spaces unlock India's full potential as a knowledge and creative entrepreneurship hub. Through strategic investments, collaborative partnerships, and the cultivation of entrepreneurial leadership, this initiative can pave the way for enterprising youth and those who cannot afford expensive commercial spaces to advance knowledge creation and pursue their goals towards economic prosperity.

15

Breaking Free from the Soft Budget Constraint: Can Kerala Embrace Economic Liberalism?

Kerala, long considered a bastion of communism in India, presents a complex narrative of evolving ideologies, vested interests, and youth aspirations. While classical Marxism and socialism appear to be weakening—particularly among younger generations—the state continues to grapple with institutional legacies shaped by both communist organization and Nehruvian state-led development.

A significant concern lies in the structure of public expenditure. A large share of state spending is directed toward salaries, pensions, and administrative commitments, often at the cost of capital investment and productive sectors. Recent state budget patterns indicate that revenue expenditure dominates fiscal allocations, with limited fiscal space for infrastructure and enterprise development. This creates conditions that resemble administratively driven systems rather than demand-driven market economies.

Such an environment can generate policy uncertainty and regulatory discretion, which in turn affects private sector confidence. Entrepreneurs, particularly in micro and small enterprises, often report difficulties navigating compliance systems that are not always aligned with the realities of emerging or informal business models.

Kerala's Political-Economic Structure

Kerala's economic structure bears certain similarities to state-led systems observed historically in parts of East and Central Europe. While the Communist Party of India (Marxist) continues to shape governance, the system itself reflects a broader coalition of ideological influences, including Nehruvian socialism represented by parties such as the Indian National Congress.

Across political formations, there is a continued emphasis on the role of the state as a central economic actor, supported by a network of cooperative institutions, public agencies, and government-aided bodies. This institutional continuity often transcends electoral cycles.

Soft Budget Constraint vs Hard Budget Constraint

The concept of soft budget constraint, developed by János Kornai, is useful in understanding Kerala's fiscal and institutional behaviour. In such systems, state-supported entities operate with the expectation of financial support irrespective of performance.

In Kerala, this is reflected in:

- Persistent support to loss-making public sector units (PSUs)
- Periodic financial restructuring or bailouts
- Limited enforcement of financial accountability mechanisms

Kerala's public debt has crossed INR 3 lakh crore in recent years, with a growing share of borrowing used to finance committed expenditure such as salaries and pensions, rather than capital formation. This pattern aligns with characteristics of a soft-budget regime.

In contrast, a hard budget constraint requires that institutions operate within clearly defined financial limits, with accountability tied to performance and outcomes.

Economic Landscape and Institutional Persistence

Kerala's economic landscape demonstrates features associated with soft-budget systems. The continued expansion of state-supported institutions, combined with borrowing-led fiscal management, constrains efficient resource allocation.

At the same time, bureaucratic processes and administrative frameworks do not always align with the requirements of a competitive, market-linked economy. While ideological positions may be evolving, institutional behaviour remains relatively unchanged.

This creates a structural paradox: ideological dilution without corresponding institutional reform.

Political Economy of Stakeholder Networks

Beyond formal structures, Kerala's economy is shaped by a network of stakeholders who derive stability from the existing system:

- Political and Administrative Elites: Including legislators, bureaucrats, and employees within state-supported institutions
- Organized Business Interests: Firms that benefit from regulatory access, land allocations, or protection from competition
- Intellectual and Cultural Institutions: Academies, think tanks, and publicly funded platforms that shape discourse

- State-supported Community Networks: Including cooperative systems and mission-based programmes such as Kudumbashree

These networks are not inherently problematic; however, their financial dependence on the state reinforces the continuation of soft-budget practices.

This configuration resembles patterns observed in late-stage socialist systems, where institutional continuity persists despite ideological shifts.

Entrepreneurial Aspirations and Structural Constraints

Kerala has witnessed a rise in entrepreneurial aspirations, particularly within the startup ecosystem. However, outside this segment, many micro and small enterprises face persistent challenges:

- Limited access to formal credit without collateral
- Complex regulatory and compliance requirements
- Weak integration into national and global value chains

At the same time, Kerala continues to experience high levels of outward migration, with remittances contributing significantly to the state's income. While remittances sustain consumption, they do not necessarily translate into productive enterprise investment within the state.

The expansion of large retail formats, including shopping malls, reflects a consumption-driven growth model. However, this has not always translated into support for local production systems. Small enterprises often struggle to compete with standardized, externally sourced goods sold through organized retail channels.

Resistance to Reform

While ideological resistance to market-oriented reforms may be declining, a more significant challenge lies in the entrenchment of institutional interests.

Similar to transitions observed in the late Soviet and Eastern European contexts, systems may persist not because of ideological conviction, but due to the strength of networks that benefit from continuity.

In Kerala, this includes:

- Public employment structures
- State-supported institutions
- Politically mediated economic access

These factors collectively slow the pace of structural reform.

Conclusion

Kerala stands at an important juncture. The weakening of ideological rigidity, combined with rising entrepreneurial aspirations, creates a window for transformation. However, without addressing the underlying institutional features associated with soft-budget constraints, structural change will remain limited.

Moving toward a more sustainable economic framework requires:

- Greater fiscal discipline
- Reorientation toward capital and enterprise development
- Strengthening of transparent and predictable regulatory systems

The transition from a consumption-led, state-supported model to a more enterprise-driven and production-oriented economy will determine Kerala's long-term trajectory.

16

Khadi and the Corporate Transition to Sustainable Consumption

Contemporary discussions on sustainability within the corporate sector remain heavily anchored in compliance frameworks—carbon disclosures, ESG reporting, and energy-efficient infrastructure. While these are necessary, they represent only one side of the sustainability equation. The other, less examined dimension lies in corporate consumption practices—what firms procure, normalize, and institutionalize within their internal systems.

This dimension is not peripheral. It is central to how markets are shaped, how enterprises grow, and how livelihoods are sustained. In this context, the question of corporate attire—often dismissed as symbolic—opens up a deeper structural opportunity. The adoption of Khadi within corporate systems is not merely a cultural choice; it is a demand-side intervention with implications for sustainability, employment, and enterprise development.

Corporate Demand and the Architecture of Inclusive Growth

Micro and small enterprises, particularly those operating in handloom and village industries, face persistent constraints in accessing stable markets. Unlike large-scale industries that benefit from capital, technology, and integrated supply chains, these sectors rely on consistent demand signals to sustain production and employment.

Corporate adoption of Khadi—through formal dress codes, institutional procurement, or branding integration—can function as a market stabilisation mechanism. Even limited adoption across sectors such as banking, hospitality, public enterprises, and services can generate predictable demand for decentralized production systems.

This has direct implications for SDG 8 (Decent Work and Economic Growth). Khadi production is inherently labour-intensive, with high employment absorption relative to capital investment. Each incremental increase in demand translates into livelihood opportunities across weaving, spinning, dyeing, and allied micro-enterprises. In this sense, corporate consumption becomes a driver of employment-led growth, rather than merely a reflection of market trends.

Reframing Sustainability: Responsible Consumption as Corporate Practice

Sustainability frameworks often prioritise production efficiencies—clean energy, reduced emissions, and resource optimization. However, SDG 12 (Responsible Consumption and Production) emphasizes that consumption patterns are equally critical. Khadi, as a product of decentralized, low-energy, and largely non-mechanised production systems, represents a model of embedded sustainability. Its integration into corporate consumption practices extends sustainability beyond reporting metrics into everyday operational behaviour.

This also aligns with SDG 13 (Climate Action), as Khadi's production processes involve significantly lower carbon intensity compared to synthetic and mass-produced textiles. By incorporating such products into institutional use, firms contribute to climate goals not through technological substitution alone, but through systemic shifts in consumption.

Enterprise Linkages and Formal Market Integration

One of the structural challenges facing micro and cottage enterprises is their limited integration into formal economic systems. Despite their contribution to employment and local economies, these sectors often remain disconnected from institutional markets.

Corporate procurement of Khadi can bridge this gap by linking informal production networks with formal demand channels. This supports SDG 9 (Industry, Innovation, and Infrastructure) by enabling small producers to participate in structured supply chains, improve quality standards, and expand market reach.

At the same time, by strengthening village industries and local production systems, such demand contributes to SDG 1 (No Poverty) and SDG 10 (Reduced Inequalities). Income generation within labour-intensive sectors has a direct impact on household stability, regional balance, and economic inclusion.

Responsible Corporate Behaviour: Beyond Compliance to Market Shaping

Responsible corporate behaviour is often interpreted narrowly as compliance with regulatory norms or participation in Corporate Social Responsibility (CSR) initiatives. However, a more substantive interpretation lies in how firms influence economic structures through their operational decisions.

Adopting Khadi as part of corporate systems reflects a shift from compliance-based responsibility to market-shaping responsibility. It signals that firms are willing to align their consumption choices with broader developmental objectives—supporting local enterprises, reducing environmental impact, and promoting inclusive growth.

This approach complements CSR but goes beyond it. Instead of treating responsibility as an external activity, it embeds it within the core functioning of the enterprise—procurement, branding, and workplace culture.

Cultural Economy and Strategic Positioning

In a changing global economic landscape, where emerging economies are redefining their position in trade and production systems, corporate identity is increasingly linked to cultural and economic context. The integration of Khadi within corporate frameworks reflects not only sustainability but also an alignment with domestic enterprise ecosystems and indigenous production systems.

Such positioning has implications for both domestic legitimacy and global differentiation. It signals a model of development that is not derivative but rooted in local capabilities, resource use patterns, and entrepreneurial traditions.

From Symbolism to Structural Transformation

The proposition to adopt Khadi as corporate attire should not be reduced to symbolism. At its core, it raises a broader economic question: Can institutional consumption be leveraged to reshape production systems in favour of labour-intensive, sustainable, and locally embedded enterprises?
In economies where MSMEs constitute the backbone of employment yet remain structurally constrained, the answer to this question carries significant policy relevance. Corporate demand, when aligned with sustainability and inclusion, can act as a powerful instrument of economic transformation.

The transition toward responsible and sustainable economic systems will not be achieved through technology alone. It requires a reorientation of consumption, production, and enterprise linkages. In that transition, corporate behaviour—down to everyday decisions such as attire—can play a far more consequential role than is currently acknowledged.

Conclusion

New Realities, New Pathways

The world is in the midst of a structural transition where long-standing assumptions about development, economic power, governance, and enterprise are steadily being redefined. The frameworks that once shaped global discourse are no longer sufficient to explain contemporary realities.

This shift is visible at multiple levels. Economic influence is becoming more distributed, with new centres of growth, innovation, and policy experimentation reshaping global dynamics. Technology is altering how states govern, how markets function, and how individuals participate in economic systems. At the same time, within enterprises, questions of ethics, trust, and sustainability are emerging as central to long-term success.

Development, therefore, cannot be understood as a fixed model or a linear progression. It is a continuous, context-driven process shaped by the interaction of policy choices, institutional capacity, technological adaptation, and human behaviour. The ability to align these elements while remaining responsive to change will determine resilience in an uncertain environment.

Equally important is the recognition that progress is not defined by growth alone. It is grounded in inclusion, dignity, and the values that guide economic activity. The balance between innovation and responsibility will shape the quality and sustainability of future outcomes.

In a changing global landscape, the need is not for rigid classifications but for adaptive and grounded approaches—ones that reflect diverse pathways and place human considerations at the centre of economic transformation.

www.ingramcontent.com/pod-product-compliance
Ingram Content Group UK Ltd.
Pitfield, Milton Keynes, MK11 3LW, UK
UKHW021400190726
13845UKWH00028B/790

9 789391 828752